PITTSBURGH
PENNSYLVANIA

A PHOTOGRAPHIC PORTRAIT

PHOTOGRAPHY BY AMY CICCONI

NARRATIVE BY CHRISTY REPEP

TWIN LIGHTS PUBLISHERS | ROCKPORT, MASSACHUSETTS

First published in the
United States of America by:

Twin Lights Publishers, Inc.
Rockport, Massachusetts 01966
Telephone: (978) 546-7398
www.twinlightspub.com

ISBN: 978-1-934907-40-5

10 9 8 7 6 5 4 3 2 1

(*opposite*)
Building Reflections

(*frontispiece*)
Point of View Sculpture

(*jacket front*)
City view from the U.S. Steel Tower

(*jacket back*)
The Golden Triangle and Duquesne Incline

Images on page 98 are used with permission
by the Carnegie Museum of Natural History.
Bottom image – background artwork by Bob
Walters and Tess Kissinger.

Images on page 99 are used with permission by
the Carnegie Museum of Art.

The image of the Cathedral of Learning, the
Cathedral of Learning name, and the University of Pittsburgh name are registered trade-
marks of the University of Pittsburgh and are
being used with permission.

Images on pages 116 and 117 are used with
permission by Kennywood®. Kennywood is a
registered trademark belonging exclusively to
Festival Fun Parks, LLC. All rights reserved.

Book design by:
SYP Design & Production, Inc.
www.sypdesign.com

Printed in China

Pittsburgh, Pennsylvania is seated majestically at the confluence of the Monongahela and Allegheny rivers and at the source of the Ohio River. Its strategic location fostered the city's growth into an industrial superpower and a major steel-manufacturing base in the early 1900s. The eventual collapse of the steel industry in the region forced the "Steel City" to overcome massive job losses and economic downturns, and to re-invent itself.

Over the past three decades, Pittsburgh has undergone a dramatic economic and cultural metamorphosis so impressive that it is widely viewed as a transformative example for other cities. Pittsburgh's essence is no longer that of a gritty, dark steel town, but rather as a vibrant, thriving urban mecca, regularly appearing in the top ranks of "most livable city" lists.

Healthcare, education, and technology are now at the core of Pittsburgh's economic ecosystem. The city's top tier universities have spawned a rapidly expanding high-tech industry, bringing with it a surge of young talent. Several of the city's oldest neighborhoods, like Lawrenceville, East Liberty, and even downtown Pittsburgh, are themselves undergoing rapid transformation and gentrification as young adults move in at impressive rates.

In addition to its economic transformation, the city has undergone a cultural revolution, and today its downtown Cultural District showcases multiple theaters, art galleries, public art projects, urban parks, and riverfront recreation spaces that draw over two million visitors to more than 1,500 events each year. Pittsburgh also enjoys a broad offering of museums where visitors can explore extensive collections of art, history, and science.

No discussion of Pittsburgh would be complete without acknowledging the city's legacy as a sports town, and the often-fanatical dedication of its residents to the city's three major professional sports teams — the Steelers (NFL), Pirates (MLB), and Penguins (NHL). Heinz Field, PNC Park, and Consol Energy Center are home to Pittsburgh's teams, and are all world-class sporting venues that have been built within the past fifteen years.

Amy Cicconi's photography takes readers on a visual journey through the evolving landscape of the city of Pittsburgh, sharing reflections of its history and compelling views of its continued vibrance.

Bridges over the Ohio River
(opposite)

With Pittsburgh's close proximity to three rivers and its abundance of hills and ravines, "The City of Bridges" has approximately 450 bridges in total. Pictured from front to back are the West End Bridge, the Ohio Connecting Railroad Bridge, and the McKees Rocks Bridge.

The Big Picture *(pages 6–7)*

A northwest aerial view from the center of the Golden Triangle provides the lay of the land. From buildings and stadiums to the rivers and the bridges that cross them, this vantage point shows much of the subject matter covered throughout this photographic journey of Pittsburgh.

Smithfield Street Bridge *(above)*

Originally built in the early 1880s, the Smithfield Street Bridge is Pittsburgh's oldest surviving river bridge. It continues to be a chief means of getting from downtown to the south shore of the Monongahela River both by vehicle and by foot. It is designated a National Historic Landmark.

Three Rivers Heritage Trail

This almost 25-mile trail that covers ground on both banks of the three rivers is the perfect way to view the city neighborhoods after which its sections are named. The Three Rivers Heritage Trail has been awarded National Recreation Trail status.

Monongahela Wharf Landing *(top)*

The "Mon Wharf" is home to a riverfront park and trail that connects to both Point State Park and the Great Allegheny Passage. With landscaping that features plants native to Western Pennsylvania, the Mon Wharf Landing is a beautiful area for Pittsburgh residents and visitors to see.

The Three Sisters *(bottom)*

Three almost identical bridges crossing the Allegheny River were given formal names honoring essential Pittsburgh residents; in the foreground: Rachel Carson (Ninth Street) Bridge; Andy Warhol (Seventh Street) Bridge; and closest to PNC Park, Roberto Clemente (Sixth Street) Bridge. They are the only trio of like bridges in the United States.

Smithfield Street Bridge *(top)*

With its two 360-foot spans, the Smithfield Street Bridge displays the longest lenticular truss spans known to remain in the United States. It is one of the first United States bridges to have trusses made of steel.

Roberto Clemente Bridge *(bottom)*

Connecting downtown to the North Shore of the Allegheny River, the Sixth Street Bridge is named after the Pittsburgh Pirates legendary right fielder Roberto Clemente. Located next to PNC Park, current home of the Pirates, it is closed to vehicular traffic during games allowing pedestrians to walk on the roadway.

Frozen Allegheny River *(pages 12–13)*

What's missing? The ships! Bitter cold and record low temperatures make the Allegheny River completely impassable.

Monongahela Incline *(above and left)*

The Monongahela Incline is the oldest incline still in service in the United States that has never ceased operation. Built in 1870, it continues to provide spectacular city views as well as to provide workers from Mt. Washington transportation to the South Shore of the Monongahela River.

Duquesne Incline *(opposite)*

Having two working inclines is a distinguishing feature of Pittsburgh. Originally built in 1877, the Duquesne Inline still operates with its original wooden cable cars that were restored in 1963. The upper station houses a gift shop full of Pittsburgh history and the view from its observation deck is breathtaking.

Pedestrian Bridge at Point State Park

Located below the Portal Bridge between the Fort Pitt and Fort Duquesne bridges, the pedestrian bridge at Point State Park crosses a shallow reflecting pool. The open lawn is the setting for many Pittsburgh events, including the Three Rivers Arts Festival.

Fort Pitt Museum *(top)*

The Fort Pitt Museum is located in a recreated bastion of Fort Pitt. The museum highlights the historical significance of Fort Pitt in the French and Indian War. The fort was completed in 1761 and was the second largest fort in North America at that time.

Fort Pitt Block House *(bottom)*

The Block House was built in 1764 as a military redoubt near Fort Pitt and, at over 250 years old, is the oldest existing structure in Western Pennsylvania. It earned Historic Landmark status from the Pittsburgh History & Landmarks Foundation in 2008.

17

Point State Park and Fountain

(opposite and bottom)

Located at the tip of the Golden Triangle, Point State Park is as well known for its fountain as for being the site where Fort Duquesne and Fort Pitt once stood. Ironically, the fountain does not draw water from the three rivers but rather from an aquifer underneath the park.

Gateway Clipper Fleet *(top)*

The Gateway Clipper Fleet is a fleet of riverboats named for a former moniker of Pittsburgh, the "Gateway to the West." The *Duchess* was built in 1965. If you have ever cruised on the Gateway Clipper Fleet's "Good Ship Lollipop" Cruise, you were most likely aboard the *Duchess*.

Mellon Square Park

(above and opposite top)

Originally opened in 1955 and rededicated in 2014, Mellon Square Park is an urban oasis built atop a downtown parking garage. The nine bronze basins of the fountain, at 3,500 pounds apiece, are the largest ever cast in one solid piece, and are home to a nightly light show.

Gateway T Station *(bottom)*

The "T" is Pittsburgh's Light Rail network. Located at Stanwix Street and Liberty Avenue, the current Gateway T Station opened in 2012 and features the mural titled *Pittsburgh Recollections* by American artist Romare Bearden.

Two Mellon Bank Center

(opposite and bottom)

Previously named the Union Trust Building, Two Mellon Bank Center is located on the site of Pittsburgh's original St. Paul Cathedral. It was commissioned in 1915 by industrialist Henry Clay Frick to serve as a shopping arcade and features an 11-story atrium topped by a stained-glass dome.

Mellon Green *(top)*

An urban park in the heart of the Golden Triangle, Mellon Green is located above the Steel Plaza T Station and is surrounded by prominent downtown Pittsburgh buildings, including BNY Mellon Center.

North Park Boathouse
(top and bottom)

North Park's lake is the largest man-made body of water in Allegheny County. The North Park Boathouse is operated by Kayak Pittsburgh, which rents various watercrafts and bicycles for riding on the trials surrounding the lake. The boathouse is also home to the Over The Bar Bicycle Café.

Hartwood Acres Park *(opposite)*

Hartwood Acres Park boasts 30 miles of trails for horse riding, hiking, biking, and cross-country skiing. The park's outdoor amphitheater holds theater productions and summer concerts. On the grounds of the park sits the Hartwood Mansion, which was completed in 1929 for the daughter of Senator William Flinn.

Aspinwall Riverfront Park (*top*)

Opened to the public in September 2015, the 11-acre Aspinwall Riverfront Park is full of surprises. This community park has walking and biking trails, gardens and a wetland area, and a stage and amphitheater. A large bronze sculpture titled *Playground* also serves as a children's slide.

Highland Park (*bottom*)

From biking and walking to sand volleyball near the swimming pool, there is something in Highland Park for everyone to do. There is even the "Super Playground" with a play phone system using underground tubes and a trolley ride.

Highland Park Fountain and Garden

One must-see attribute of Highland Park is the park entrance with its Victorian garden and reflecting pool with fountain. Stone steps lead to one of the city's main reservoirs, which is surrounded by a stunning walking / running track.

Law Enforcement Officers Memorial *(left and right)*

Originally dedicated in 1996, the memorial includes a statue of an officer and his K9 partner with the inscription "Ever Watchful," a black granite wall inscribed with the names of fallen officers, and an old call box painted red and blue, complete with granite block inscribed with "Final Call."

Soldiers & Sailors Memorial Hall & Museum

Soldiers & Sailors honors servicemen and women from all military branches. American history is told through artifacts from US military personnel. The Gettysburg Room showcases African American experiences from enslavement through today, and the Hall of Valor honors American heroes.

The Pennsylvanian *(above and left)*

Now known as The Pennsylvanian, the former Penn Train Station serves mainly as a luxury condominium building. The rotunda was originally the carriage entrance to Penn Station and features a large coffered dome with central skylight. Amtrak still runs trains out of the basement.

Vietnam Veterans' Monument *(opposite)*

This moving memorial shows life-sized soldiers reuniting with their families. The canopy covering the statues is an inverted hibiscus pod, an Asiatic symbol of rebirth and regeneration, symbolizing the warrior's return to peace. The Vietnamese words for "grant us peace" are inscribed on the inside of the dome.

Water Steps *(pages 32–33)*

Water Steps is a public fountain near PNC Park. Water runs over large sandstone blocks resembling steps of varying heights. A must-see attraction for kids and adults alike, Water Steps is a large, refreshing interactive fountain and a popular destination on hot summer days.

Korean War Memorial *(above)*

Originally dedicated in 1999, the Korean War Memorial is shaped and positioned to capture sunlight. The play of light and shadow evokes memories and emotions both unique to the individual visitor and common with their fellow man.

World War II Memorial

(opposite, top and bottom)

The World War II Memorial includes panels of glass and granite that describe the war, the region's role in the conflict, and the sacrifices of local veterans. The interior is devoted to the local history while the exterior describes the story of the war around the world.

THE WAR BEGINS

In Germany, unresolved grievances resulting from the negotiated end of World War I contributed to the rise of Adolf Hitler and control of the government by the Nazi Party. Having re-armed fully, Germany marched unopposed into Austria in 1938 and seized control of Czechoslovakia later that year. But not until after the invasion of Poland in 1939 did England and France begin their military resistance to the continuing aggression of Germany and its Axis ally, Italy.

The war in Europe began poorly for the Allies. Fascist armies swept eastward across Poland, occupied Norway and The Netherlands, defeated English and French forces in Belgium and France, and moved south to control North Africa. Britain avoided invasion only by heroically maintaining air supremacy over the English Channel. And it fought virtually alone until mid-1941 when Germany attacked Russia in violation of a treaty between those nations.

In Asia, events involving Japan were eerily similar to those occurring in Europe. That fuel-starved nation began its imperialistic march in 1931 by seizing Manchuria for its abundant coal and oil reserves. Soon, much of China was under the invaders' control. In 1941, Japan occupied Indochina, announced an alliance with Germany and Italy, and laid plans both to extend its military presence deep into the Pacific and limit America's capacity to interfere as those operations were carried out.

Point of View Sculpture *(top)*

One-time allies George Washington and Seneca leader Guyasuta would later fight on opposing sides in the French and Indian War. The *Point of View* sculpture depicts an October 1770 meeting at which they discussed their differing opinions on the fate of the area that would become Pittsburgh.

USS Requin *(bottom)*

The USS *Requin* submarine was built during World War II but never saw action in that conflict. It underwent three conversions to become the first US Navy radar picket submarine. Today, it is a featured attraction at the Carnegie Science Center, educating visitors about life onboard a military submersible.

Allegheny Observatory *(opposite)*

The Allegheny Observatory is a focal point of Riverview Park. In the 1850s businessmen built the observatory for what was then the third largest telescope in the world. Now operated by the University of Pittsburgh, the observatory is a private research laboratory, although there is a public tour program.

Aerial View Oakland

An urban and diverse neighborhood, Oakland is home to universities, museums, and hospitals, as well as an abundance of shopping, restaurants, and recreational activities. Pictured in the foreground is the William Pitt Union, the student union building of the University of Pittsburgh; in the distance is the Golden Triangle.

EQT Plaza (top)

In May 2015, the EQT Plaza courtyard reopened. The space totals more than 7,500 square feet and features tables and seating, bike racks, and various trees and flowers. The Penelope Jencks bronze sculptures are said to honor the music community, which plays a major role in the nearby Cultural District.

Agnes R. Katz Plaza (bottom)

Also known as Eyeball Park, this half-acre public plaza officially opened in 1999 in Pittsburgh's downtown Cultural District. In the middle of 32 linden trees stands a 25-foot-tall bronze fountain featuring gently trickling water. The water is heated, allowing it to flow year round.

The Builders Sculpture *(opposite)*

Standing at the opening walkway to Allegheny Landing, *The Builders* bronze sculpture was commissioned by the Mellon-Stuart construction company, which provided photographs of actual employees on which the figures are based. Dedicated in 1984, it is a tribute to those who made Pittsburgh's "renaissance" construction projects a success.

The Workers Sculpture *(top)*

These steel "workers" are made of steel once used in construction of Pittsburgh's Hot Metal Bridge. The sculpture, dedicated in 2011, celebrates the rich industrial steel heritage of the "Steel City " but also serves as a link between the past and Pittsburgh's emergence as an artistic powerhouse.

Edgar Thomson Plant *(bottom)*

The Edgar Thomson Plant is one of four facilities that make up Mon Valley Works of U.S. Steel Corporation. Steel slabs from this plant are used in products including appliances, buildings, and automotive vehicles. Mon Valley Works has the ability to produce 2.9 million net tons of raw steel annually.

PPG Place *(above and opposite)*

This six-building office complex centers around One PPG Place, which, at 635 feet, ranks as the third tallest building in Pittsburgh. Named for PPG Industries, the anchor tenant that initiated the project, all six buildings have a matching design, made of nearly one million square feet of reflective glass.

Benedum-Trees Building *(right)*

The 19-story Benedum-Trees Building, built in 1905, is part of the Fourth Avenue Historic District in downtown Pittsburgh. The beautiful façade, with its three-story Corinthian columns, uses a light colored granite, white brick, and terra cotta; and is rivaled by a lobby adorned with bronze and marble.

PPG Place Plaza Fountain

The fountain at PPG Place, with no barrier between the water and the rest of the plaza, is a favorite meeting spot. Take a run through the fifteen-foot-high pulsating spouts or visit during the winter months when the plaza is transformed into an ice-skating rink.

Yoga in the Square

From the weekly farmer's market to the seasonal Holiday Village shops, Market Square plays host for many events year round. Just one of the many popular events is Yoga in the Square; on summer Sunday mornings community yoga classes are provided free of charge.

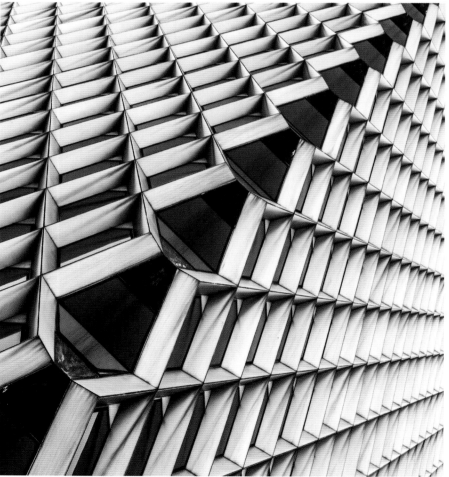

Alcoa Corporate Center *(above)*

A global leader in lightweight metals technology, engineering, and manufacturing, Alcoa is the world's third largest aluminum producer. Its corporate center moved to a six-story aluminum and glass structure in 1998. Its wave-form glass façade was designed to reflect river movement.

United Steel Workers Building *(left)*

Originally built for IBM, this was the first structure to use steel of three different strength levels and the first exterior space frame building ever constructed with a diagonal-grid load-bearing steel wall. This 13-story building has only eight ground anchors supporting the wall structure.

Gateway Center *(opposite)*

Part of the Pittsburgh Renaissance Historic District, Gateway Center is an office complex whose first three buildings were designed by the same firm who completed the Thomas Jefferson Memorial. It is a focal point of the Western Pennsylvania Conservancy for the "greening" of downtown.

Allegheny County Courthouse
(above, left, and opposite)

Designed by Henry Hobson Richardson, the courthouse is known for its Romanesque style. Features include a courtyard, a tower, and multiple dormers. Five murals painted by Vincent Nesbert, including *Justice*, are prominent on the second floor. The courthouse was designated a National Historic Landmark in 1976.

·IN·MEMORY·OF·
HENRY·HOBSON·RICHARDSON
·1838· ·ARCHITECT· ·1886·

City-County Building *(above and left)*

Opened in 1917, the City-County Building was designed by Henry Hornbostel. The columns in its main hall that support a vaulted terra cotta tile ceiling are almost 50 feet high. Outside the Grant Street entrance, a commemorative statue of former Pittsburgh mayor Richard Caliguiri stands ever watchful.

Frick Building *(opposite)*

Henry Clay Frick's building was purportedly built taller than the Carnegie Building, which was demolished in 1952, so that the offices of Frick's rival, Andrew Carnegie, would be shrouded in shadows. The lobby of the Frick Building features bronze lions and a stained-glass window by John La Farge illustrating *Fortune and Her Wheel*.

August Wilson Center for African American Culture *(opposite top)*

Named for the native Pittsburgh playwright, this architecturally stunning cultural center is dedicated to celebrating the contributions of African Americans to American theater, music, and art. The center has an educational area, flexible exhibit space, a music café, and performing arts theater.

Kaufmann's Clock *(opposite bottom)*

The original Kaufmann's clock was installed in 1887 as a freestanding four-faced clock. When the department store expanded in 1913, the current clock was installed. Kaufmann's became Macy's but the clock remained and is a Pittsburgh Historical Landmark. In 2015, Macy's closed its downtown Pittsburgh location after 128 years.

Omni William Penn Hotel
(left and right)

The final building endeavor of Henry Clay Frick, the hotel boasts almost 600 guest rooms and suites and over 52,000 square feet of meeting and event space. Opened in 1916, the William Penn became a major convention facility when the Grant Street Annex was completed in 1929.

Fourth Avenue Historic District
(above and right)

Fourth Avenue was the city's financial center around the turn of the 20th century. This historic district showcases buildings designed by more than a dozen distinguished architects. Pictured above is part of the Times Building façade, and pictured right is the Burke Building, the oldest business building in the city.

Liberty Avenue *(opposite)*

Buildings along downtown's Liberty Avenue, part of the Penn-Liberty Historic District, are some of the most nearly intact portions of the city's late 19th- and early 20th-century retailing district. In addition to beautifully restored performance halls and hotels, the area includes renovated commercial buildings containing galleries, schools, restaurants, and residences.

Joy of Life Sculpture

Sculpted by Virgil Cantini in 1969, *Joy of Life* is a Cor-Ten steel sculpture originally located at East Liberty Mall. In 1990 it was moved to its current location at Whitfield Street and Baum Boulevard. East Liberty Presbyterian Church, also known as the "Cathedral of Hope," is in the background.

Dollar Bank

Part of the Fourth Avenue Historic District, the original Dollar Bank building was designed by Isaac Hobbs and built in 1870 and ornamented with two lions carved in 1871 by Max Kohler. The original lions were restored and moved inside in 2010 and the external pedestals now showcase replicated lions.

PNC Green Wall *(opposite)*

The PNC Financial Services Group, Inc. commissioned this green wall as an innovative way to make its headquarters building more energy-efficient. It is estimated that each of the 602 panels, with 24 plants in each 2x2-square-foot space, will offset the carbon footprint of one person.

Allegheny Cemetery *(top and bottom)*

Incorporated in 1844, Allegheny Cemetery is one of the oldest rural cemeteries in America. The Gatehouse at the Butler Street entrance was listed on the National Register of Historic Places in 1974. The cemetery hosts events such as musical performances and parades.

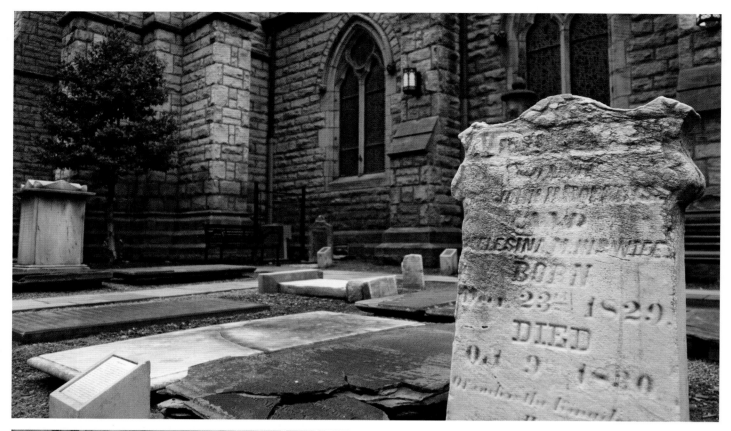

Trinity Cathedral (*above and left*)

Located in the heart of downtown Pittsburgh, the Trinity Cathedral is an Episcopal Church and the cathedral for the Episcopal Diocese of Pittsburgh. The site was once also used as a cemetery and has some of the oldest marked graves inland from the East Coast.

St. Paul Cathedral (*opposite*)

St. Paul Cathedral is the Mother Church of the Diocese of Pittsburgh. Originally located downtown, when city residents began moving their homes to outside areas, the cathedral was rebuilt in the Oakland section of Pittsburgh in 1906 at a cost of $1.1 million, including $205,000 for the land.

Smithfield United Church of Christ *(above and left)*

Smithfield United Church of Christ is the oldest organized church in the city of Pittsburgh and dates back to 1782. Today, it is an inclusive congregation that serves the downtown area in multiple ways, including a severe weather emergency shelter and a walk-in ministry food pantry.

First Presbyterian Church
(opposite, top and bottom)

First Presbyterian Church of Pittsburgh was incorporated on September 29, 1787. In 1903, the cornerstone was laid for the present building. The sanctuary has 14 memorial stained-glass windows, 13 of which were designed and installed by Tiffany Studios. The pipe organ has over 4,400 pipes and 77 ranks.

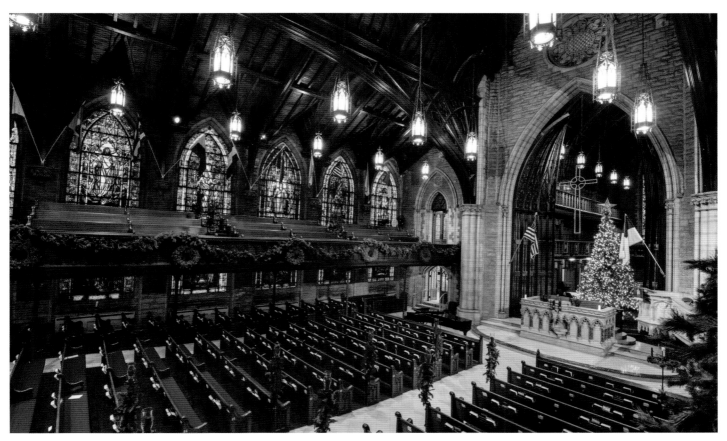

Rodef Shalom Temple

(above and left)

The Rodef Shalom Temple in Shadyside was architected by Henry Hornbostel and is a National Register of Historic Places landmark. On its grounds sits the Biblical Botanical Garden, as well as a series of bronze sculpted figures titled, *Procession I*, by noted sculptor Elbert Weinberg.

Heinz Memorial Chapel *(above)*

Heinz Memorial Chapel, located on the Oakland campus of the University of Pittsburgh, is a nondenominational chapel given to the university by the H. J. Heinz family. Architect Charles Z. Klauder, who also designed the University's Cathedral of Learning, designed the two buildings using the same neo-Gothic architecture.

Immaculate Heart of Mary Church *(right)*

The Immaculate Heart of Mary Church, located in Pittsburgh's Polish Hill section, is one of the city's oldest churches. This historic church's architecture is considered to be in the "Polish Cathedral style," and is modeled after St. Peter's Basilica in Rome.

The Church Brew Works *(top)*

The Church Brew Works is a popular brewpub in Pittsburgh's Lawrenceville neighborhood that is set in a restored Roman Catholic church. Aspects of the church are still evident. For example, the altar, which houses the steel and copper tanks of the brew house, serves as the centerpiece of the restaurant.

Grand Concourse *(bottom and opposite)*

The elegant Grand Concourse Restaurant is housed in the former Pittsburgh and Lake Erie Railroad Station, on the city's South Shore, in the Station Square shopping and entertainment complex. The restaurant's grand staircase leads to the main dining room, with cathedral stained-glass ceilings and opulent marble columns.

Liberty Avenue Musicians (*top*)

These three 15-foot-tall concrete musicians in Pittsburgh's Cultural and Historic districts by artist James Simon pay tribute to the musical legacy of the city of Pittsburgh. The trio of musicians and the sleepy dog at their feet seem to be happily lost in the music that they are creating.

Heinz Hall for the Performing Arts (*bottom and opposite*)

Majestic Heinz Hall for the Performing Arts serves as the cornerstone for the Cultural District of Pittsburgh. This grand showplace, renowned as a world-class concert hall, is home to the Pittsburgh Symphony Orchestra and hosts a wide variety of musical events and Broadway shows each year.

Benedum Center *(above)*

This popular Pittsburgh Cultural District performing arts center has a rich history as a top entertainment venue, hosting big bands, rock legends, movies, and Broadway shows. After a $43 million restoration, the Benedum is one of the few theaters in the U.S. large enough to stage full-cast, first-run Broadway shows.

Cultural District *(left)*

The Pittsburgh Cultural District is a 14-block neighborhood in the heart of Pittsburgh's Golden Triangle that is the showcase of the city's evolving arts revitalization efforts. The Cultural District features a variety of theaters, offering thousands of shows annually, as well as numerous art galleries, restaurants, and retail shops.

Firstside Historic District *(top)*

The historic Firstside District comprises an area of Pittsburgh's stone-paved banks along Monongahela River, which were a favorite stop for wharf boats and steamships in the 1800s. The historic district designation represents this area's role in the economic development of Pittsburgh's river trade, as well as its architectural significance.

Remnants of Yesteryear *(bottom)*

Although Pittsburgh is considered the Steel City, much of its architecture is made from brick and masonry. Throughout the city, remnants of "ghost signs"— advertisements from years gone by — are present everywhere, as old architecture mingles with new. These faded messages serve as reminders of the city's rich history.

Strip District *(top and bottom)*

Pittsburgh's Strip District, a weekend hot spot, is a half-mile-square shopping district filled with ethnic grocers, produce stands, sidewalk vendors, and meat and fish markets. Robert Wholey & Company is among the most iconic purveyors, offering a vast selection of fresh seafood, meat, and poultry.

The Two Andys Mural *(opposite)*

The Two Andys mural, painted by Sarah Zeffiro and Tom Mosser, is on Smithfield Street, above Weiner World. The mural depicts two famous Pittsburghers getting a makeover — industrialist Andrew Carnegie and pop artist Andy Warhol, who is seen reading *Fences* by Pittsburgh native and Pulitzer Prize winner August Wilson.

East Carson Street (above and left)

East Carson Street runs through the city's South Side and is well known as a hot spot for weekend nightlife. Along this 15-block stretch, a National Historic District, Victorian-style buildings house a plethora of bars, restaurants, eclectic stores, theater and live music venues, tattoo shops, and art galleries.

House Poem (opposite top)

House Poem is one of four houses transformed into public art projects on Sampsonia Way on Pittsburgh's North Side. A project by City of Asylum, a grass-roots organization providing exiled writers from around the world with housing, the Chinese-calligraphy covered home called House Poem was created by Huang Xiang.

Randyland (opposite bottom)

Located in the Mexican War Streets district of Pittsburgh's North Side, Randyland was once the home of a speakeasy and was later converted by artist and colorful character Randy Gilson into one of the most colorful spectacles in the city, using paints, plants, plastic animals, and yard sale treasures.

Bayernhof Museum *(top and bottom)*

The Bayernhof Museum showcases an extensive collection of rare automatic musical instruments in a 19,000-square-foot residence built by Pittsburgh businessman Charles Brown II. The mansion, with its unique features, including an indoor cave and secret passages, houses antique music boxes, pipe organs, and other rarities.

Mexican War Streets *(opposite)*

The Mexican War Streets is a historic district in Pittsburgh's Central North Side neighborhood, filled with beautifully restored row houses and tree-lined streets and alleyways. One of the city's oldest neighborhoods, many of the Mexican War Street's Victorian-style buildings date from the mid-19th century.

Negley Gwinner-Harter House *(above)*

Mansions like the Negley Gwinner-Harter House can be found on "Millionaire's Row" in Shadyside, home to many great turn-of-the-century industrialists and financiers. Originally built in 1871 by William Negley, the home was damaged by fire in 1987 and saved from demolition by a restoration in 1995.

Moreland-Hoffstot Mansion *(right)*

The Moreland-Hoffstot Mansion is another home on Millionaire's Row on Fifth Avenue in Shadyside, and was built in 1914 by iron and steel magnate Andrew Moreland. The house is a second-generation copy of the Grand Trianon at Versailles, which Louis XIV built for his mistress.

The Inn on the Mexican War Streets *(opposite)*

This magnificent inn was once the town home of financier and department store baron Russell H. Boggs. The mansion and its carriage house were built in 1888 under the direction of H. H. Richardson, who also designed the Allegheny County Courthouse.

Frick Art and Historical Center
(top and bottom)

The Frick Art and Historical Center is a complex of museums and historical buildings located amidst beautifully landscaped gardens in the residential East End. Devoted to the interpretation of the life and times of industrialist and art collector Henry Clay Frick, the museum exhibits fine and decorative art.

Clayton House, Frick Art & Historical Center

The centerpiece of The Frick Art & Historical Center is the Clayton House, the beautifully restored Victorian home of Henry Clay Frick. Deemed a "triumph of restoration" by *Architectural Digest*, the Clayton is filled with furniture and artifacts that are over 90% original to the family.

Mellon Park Fountain

Banker and philanthropist Richard Mellon's estate was perhaps the biggest mansion in Pittsburgh, but was torn down just 31 years after its completion. The mansion's impressive garden was converted to a city park, and a beautiful fountain stands as a focal point near the former estate's "Walled Garden."

Pittsburgh Botanic Garden

The Pittsburgh Botanic Garden is the region's first comprehensive outdoor botanic garden focusing on hardy plants adaptable to the soils and climate in Western Pennsylvania. The sprawling 460-acre garden is situated on abandoned mining land.

Hygeia Statue *(left)*

Hygeia, the Greek Goddess of health, daughter of Asclepius, the Greek god of medicine, stands near the Aquatic Gardens in the Phipps Conservatory and Botanical Gardens. The statue, by Giuseppe Moretti, was commissioned by the Allegheny County Medical Society to honor their members who served in World War I.

Phipps Conservatory and Botanical Gardens *(right)*

This great steel and glass Victorian greenhouse is set amidst one of Pittsburgh's largest greenspaces, Schenley Park. Housing formal gardens and various species of exotic plants, Phipps Conservatory stands as a cultural and architectural centerpiece of the city's Oakland neighborhood.

Phipps Conservatory and Botanical Gardens *(above and pages 86–87)*

Deemed one of the "greenest" facilities in the world, the entrance pavilion of the conservatory has silver-level LEED certification. The "green" design of the Welcome Center and neo-Victorian dome complement the original Lord and Burnham conservatory and reflect its mission to connect people with nature.

La Roche College *(above)*

The majestic Providence Heights building on the 80-acre campus of La Roche College dominates the landscape of the North Hills of Pittsburgh. Providence Heights was designed and built in 1927 in the architectural style of a Bavarian castle.

University of Pittsburgh *(left)*

The University of Pittsburgh, commonly referred to as "Pitt," is a nationally and internationally top-ranked public university. Pitt's main campus is comprised of approximately 132 urban acres located in Pittsburgh's Oakland neighborhood. The university's mascot is the panther; the bronze *Millennium Panther* is one of a number of panther sculptures on campus.

Walking to the Sky *(opposite)*

Carnegie Mellon University is home to *Walking to the Sky*, a stainless steel and resin artwork by CMU graduate Jonathan Borofsky. The artwork features human figures walking up a cylindrical pole in the direction of the sky, while onlookers are standing at the base gazing up at the surreal scene.

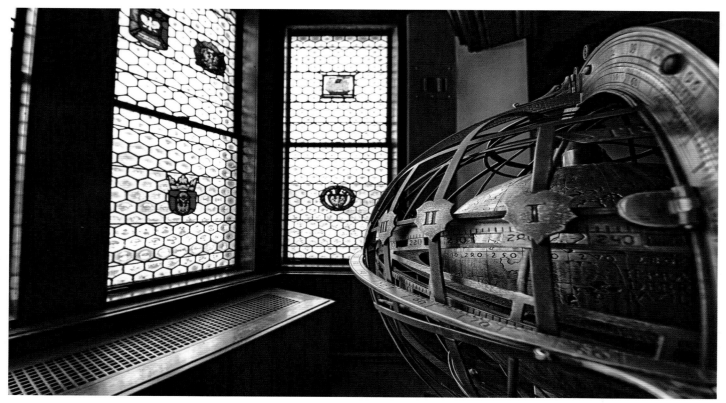

Nationality Rooms *(above and left)*

The Nationality Rooms are a collection of 29 classrooms in the University of Pittsburgh's Cathedral of Learning representing the ethnic groups that helped build the city of Pittsburgh. Designated as a Historic Landmark, many of the rooms are used as functional classrooms. Shown here are the Polish and Chinese rooms.

Cathedral of Learning
(opposite and pages 92–93)

Pitt's Cathedral of Learning is the centerpiece of the university's main campus in the Oakland neighborhood. The 42-story Gothic Revival structure's magnificent four-story-tall Commons Room is touted as one of the "great architectural fantasies of the twentieth century" due to its incredible use of the Gothic style.

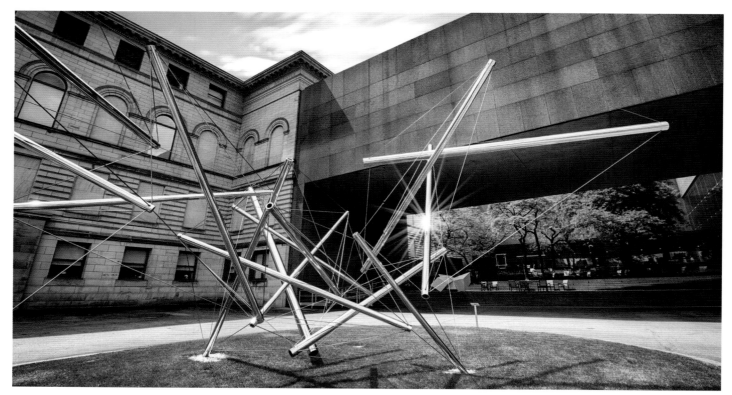

Forest Devil Sculpture *(top)*

This steel sculpture by Kenneth Snelson, located outside the Carnegie Museum of Art, is an excellent example of "tensegrity," a combination of the words "tension" and "integrity." Its polished steel tubes and aircraft cables are held together by a precise combination of opposing forces that establish equilibrium.

Carnegie Mellon University *(bottom)*

Carnegie Mellon University, founded in 1900 and located in the Oakland neighborhood, is a top-tier global research university that is known for its programs in science and technology. CMU has played an integral role in Pittsburgh's successful economic transformation from a steel town to a booming high-tech center.

Christopher Columbus *(opposite)*

Frank Vittor's 50-foot-tall bronze statue of Christopher Columbus was erected in Schenley Park in 1958 after a fifty-year fundraising effort. Vittor, a Pittsburgher originally born in Italy, studied under August Rodin in France and taught sculpture at the Carnegie Institute of Technology, now Carnegie Mellon University.

Mary Schenley Memorial Fountain

The Mary Schenley Memorial Fountain, also known as *A Song to Nature*, is by artist Victor David Brenner. This beautiful work features Pan, the Greek God of shepherds, and a nymph playing a lyre. The fountain sits in Schenley Plaza, honoring Mary Schenley, who donated the land for Schenley Park.

Westinghouse Memorial

Schenley Park is also home to the Westinghouse Memorial, a bronze and granite monument commemorating engineer George Westinghouse. The memorial consists of a statue of a schoolboy representing "The Spirit of the American Youth," who looks on and draws inspiration from three panels depicting the life of George Westinghouse.

Carnegie Museum of Natural History *(top and bottom)*

Dippy, a sculpture of a Diplodocus dinosaur, greets visitors at the Carnegie Museum of Natural History in the Oakland neighborhood. Ranked among the top U.S. natural history museums, it is known for its dinosaurs and maintains an extraordinary collection of 22 million objects and scientific specimens.

Carnegie Museum of Art

Carnegie Museum of Art, known as the first U.S. museum of contemporary art, upholds founder Andrew Carnegie's vision of collecting the "Old Masters of tomorrow." Depicted is the soaring three-story Grand Staircase, which integrates a mural by John White Alexander representing progress achieved through hard work and industrial power.

National Aviary *(top, left and above)*

The National Aviary is America's largest independent aviary and is the only aviary awarded honorary "National" status by the U.S. Congress. The aviary's large walk-through exhibits feature hundreds of species of birds from around the world in their natural habitats, many of which are threatened or endangered in the wild.

Pittsburgh Zoo and PPG Aquarium *(top, right and above)*

Situated on 77 acres in Pittsburgh's Highland Park neighborhood, the Pittsburgh Zoo and PPG Aquarium features thousands of mammals, birds, reptiles, fish, and amphibians, many roaming in naturalistic habitats. It is one of a select few major zoo and aquarium combinations in the United States.

ToonSeum (above and right)

Pittsburgh's downtown is home to ToonSeum, one of only a handful of museums in the U.S. dedicated exclusively to art from comic strips, graphic novels, comic books, and animated film. This small boutique-style museum exhibits more than 100 pieces of art at any given time, rotating exhibits every few months.

Mattress Factory (opposite)

The Mattress Factory is a museum of contemporary and experimental art that one can "get into," with room-sized environments housing works created by in-residence artists from around the world. The museum, a recognized leader in site-specific installations, video, and performance art, is located in the North Side's Mexican War Streets.

"Arch" Robot Made of Bridges

Arch, a robot made of replicas of Pittsburgh's many bridges created by sculptor Glenn Kaino, represents "a bridge between the past, present and future of the region." This 20-foot-tall Transformer-like sculpture, constructed from steel and fiberglass, now resides in the landside terminal at the Pittsburgh International Airport.

Mr. Rogers Statue

Fred Rogers, one of the most iconic and beloved figures in children's television, is remembered with a bronze statue called *Tribute to Children* on Pittsburgh's North Shore. This 11-foot-tall bronze figure created by sculptor Robert Berks depicts Rogers in his classic pose — sitting down and tying his sneakers.

Art Rooney Statue

Art Rooney, the highly revered founder of the Pittsburgh Steelers, is memorialized with a bronze statue located outside Heinz Field, next to "Art Rooney Avenue." The statue, created by Raymond Kaskey, is one the few remaining relics from Pittsburgh's Three Rivers Stadium, the predecessor to PNC Park and Heinz Field.

Heinz Field

Heinz Field, located along the Ohio River on Pittsburgh's North Shore, serves as the home to the Pittsburgh Steelers NFL and the University of Pittsburgh Panthers football teams. The stadium incorporates 12,000 tons of steel into its design, a nod to the city of Pittsburgh's history of steel production.

Senator John Heinz History Center *(above)*

Located in Pittsburgh's Strip District, this is Pennsylvania's largest history museum and is an affiliate of the Smithsonian Institution. Its six floors feature traveling and long-term exhibitions that preserve regional history and present the American experience with a Western Pennsylvania connection.

Western Pennsylvania Sports Museum *(opposite top and bottom)*

The Western Pennsylvania Sports Museum, located on the second floor of the Senator John Heinz History Center, celebrates the region's evolution as a leader in sports with more than 70 interactive exhibits. The area's passion for sports from football to baseball and hockey to golf are showcased.

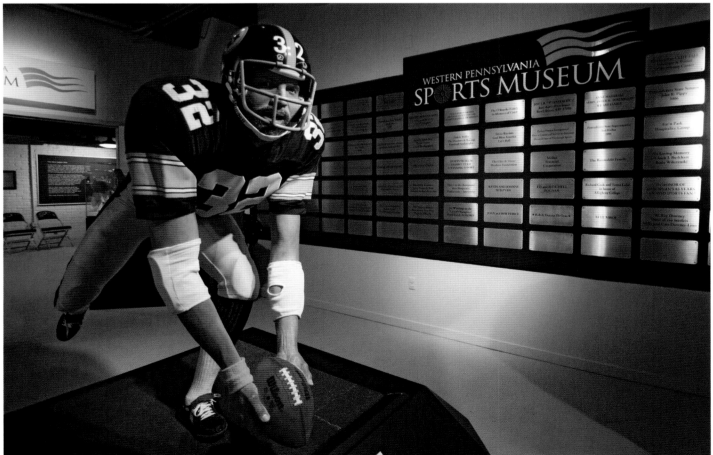

PNC Park *(opposite)*

PNC Park's intimate design places the highest seat just 88 feet from the field, giving every fan in the park an ideal line of sight. The blue color of the seats is a replica of "Forbes Field Blue," a carryover from the city's beloved former ballpark that was in Oakland.

PNC Park *(top and bottom)*

PNC Park, home of the Pittsburgh Pirates, sits along the city's Allegheny River shoreline. This dynamic urban sports venue provides scenic views of the downtown skyline and riverfront. A classic-style ballpark, PNC Park embraces the spirit of early ballpark originals such as Forbes Field, Wrigley Field, and Fenway Park.

Roberto Clemente *(above, left)*

Roberto Clemente is arguably the most revered athlete in Pittsburgh's sports history. "The Great One" is memorialized in a 12-foot bronze statue outside PNC Park. His likeness, in an action pose, sits upon a circular timeline with significant dates from his life aligned with the bases on a diamond.

Bill Mazeroski Statue *(above, right)*

A bronze statue outside PNC Park on Mazeroski Way depicts the likeness of the legendary Pirate second baseman rounding the bases after his famous home run in the bottom of the ninth inning that enabled the Pirates to beat the New York Yankees in the 1960 World Series.

Willie Stargell *(left)*

Willie "Pops" Stargell, the heart of the Pittsburgh Pirates' 1970s championship teams, is immortalized in bronze outside PNC Park's left field gate. The statue, by local artist Susan Wagner, depicts the Hall of Fame slugger waiting for a pitch, with his bat drawn back impossibly far in typical Stargell style.

CONSOL Energy Center

CONSOL Energy Center, home of the Pittsburgh Penguins, is the first LEED gold certified NHL facility in North America. Mario Lemieux, arguably the most admired Penguin in history, is immortalized in bronze on Centre Avenue. *Le Magnifique* depicts Lemieux breaking through two defenders on his way to scoring a goal.

Three Rivers Regatta *(above and left)*

The annual Three Rivers Regatta is a grand celebration of Pittsburgh's rivers, highlighted each summer by a Formula One power boat race. Pittsburgh's regatta is America's largest inland regatta and traditionally includes food, entertainment, family-friendly events, jet ski stunts, and an "Anything That Floats Race."

Pittsburgh Vintage Grand Prix

(above and right)

The Pittsburgh Vintage Grand Prix, held annually in Schenley Park, is the nation's largest vintage sports car racing event, and the only one that is run on actual city streets. The course, considered to be one of the most challenging in the world, traverses Schenley Park's Serpentine Drive.

Kennywood® *(top and bottom)*

Pittsburgh's Kennywood amusement park is a familiar tradition for many Pittsburgh area residents. A fun family destination since 1898, many of Kennywood's original vintage features remain in operation today. The park's extensive Kiddieland area, and the 1930s classic auto race ride are both long-standing favorites for young children.

The Thunderbolt

This classic wooden roller coaster, dubbed the "King of Coasters" by the *New York Times* in the 1970s, shocks riders with an incredible plunge immediately upon leaving the station. In 2014, the Thunderbolt was designated a historical Coaster Landmark, becoming the third of Kennywood's coasters to receive this honor.

Carnegie Science Center *(top)*

The Carnegie Science Center, situated on the city's North Shore, offers hands-on science exhibits, a planetarium, and the world's largest permanent robotics exhibit. The E-Motion Cone atop the science center utilizes a computerized lighting system to display different colored lights, signaling the weather forecast for the coming day.

Andy Warhol Museum *(bottom)*

The Andy Warhol Museum on the North Shore is dedicated to the works of Pittsburgh-born artist Andy Warhol. The museum is one of the most comprehensive museums dedicated to a single artist in the world and houses an extensive collection tracing Warhol's work from illustrator to pop icon.

Original Hot Dog Shop (top)

Affectionately known by locals as "The O," the Original Hot Dog Shop in Oakland is known for its hot dogs and large portions of twice-cooked french fries. A Pittsburgh tradition for more than 50 years, The O's hot dogs have been highly ranked by *Gourmet Magazine* and *The New York Times*.

Fireworks (bottom)

Pittsburgh's riverfronts serve as a spectacular setting for year-round fireworks displays. Whether it is after a Pirates game, Fourth of July, Light Up Night, or during the Three Rivers Regatta, thousands of Pittsburghers flock to the shores of the Monongahela, Allegheny, and Ohio rivers to take in the colorful show.

Mount Washington View
(pages 120–121)

USA Today has ranked the panoramic view of the city of Pittsburgh from high atop Mount Washington as one of the world's best skyline views. From this vantage point, visitors enjoy expansive views of downtown Pittsburgh, and the city's three rivers and the many bridges crossing them.

Children's Museum of Pittsburgh

(above)

More Light, an art installation featuring hundreds of pink and orange streamers, is suspended over the ceiling of the Studio space at the Children's Museum of Pittsburgh. The museum's 80,000 square feet of space allows children to have an array of hands-on play and learning experiences.

Children's Museum of Pittsburgh

(opposite)

The museum's main building connects the historic Allegheny Post Office and the former Buhl Planetarium. Visitors can see a Foucault pendulum — a device that demonstrates the rotation of the earth — that was originally an attraction in the grand hallway of the old Buhl Planetarium.

DO NOT TOUCH
the Pendulum

Children's Museum of Pittsburgh
(top)

The museum's three-story, steel and glass main structure has many sustainable design features, earning it the distinction of becoming the first LEED-certified children's museum in the country. Its evening illumination is symbolic of children's advocacy and the revitalization of the historic North Side.

Primitive Science and Modern Science *(bottom)*

Figures *Primitive Science* and *Modern Science* are two of six bronze reliefs on the exterior of the former Buhl Planetarium. *Primitive Science* features a Native American surrounded by fire and medicinal plants, while *Modern Science* depicts a researcher with chemistry, physics, and geography objects.

Navigation and Enlightenment Statue *(opposite)*

Navigation and Enlightenment is a granite sculpture that originally adorned the top of Pittsburgh's Fourth Avenue Post Office. When the building was razed in the 1960s, it found a new home in the Old Post Office Museum's Artifact Garden, where many additional artifacts are also located.

Olde Allegheny Community Gardens

The Olde Allegheny Community Gardens are nestled amidst the densely packed Victorian houses on the Mexican War Streets in Pittsburgh's North Side. Each participant gets one of 40 plots to grow whatever they want in one of these two organic, urban gardens that were started in the 1980s.

Piazza Lavoro and Mythic Source

This two-part sculpture installation by Ned Smyth sits on an upper overlook of Allegheny Landing, Pittsburgh's first public sculpture park along the Allegheny River. *Piazza Lavoro*, four large façades featuring mosaic renderings of laborers at work, surrounds the column *Mythic Source*, which is a celebration of water.